War of the Two Kings

Oliver Cromwell's solution to the Irish question is known as the Cromwellian Settlement. Through this act Irish Catholic lands were confiscated in order to pay the soldiers and creditors of Cromwell's New Model Army, which repressed the Confederate Wars of 1641-1652 in Ireland. Furthermore, it prohibited Catholics from holding public offices or bearing arms. No Catholic could vote, or so much as carry a sword.

Soon after Cromwell's death the Stuarts were restored to the throne of England under Charles II in 1660. Charles attempted to impose religious toleration, but was opposed by the Anglicans in parliament who had supported his restoration, and backed down. However, Catholics in Ireland enjoyed some toleration under Charles' rule. This came to an end in 1679 when Titus Oates' revelations of a supposed 'Popish Plot' sparked anti-Catholic hysteria. The Irish who had fought for Charles' father expected to be compensated, and their lands returned. Only a few 'Old English' Catholic Royalists ever recovered their estates.

After Charles' death his brother James succeeded to the throne of England, as James II. Unlike his brother James was an open and devoted Catholic. He allowed Catholics to hold some of the highest offices in England despite Anglican opposition. The birth of a son by James' second wife agitated matters in England. Anglicans feared a permanent Catholic dynasty and the establishment of an absolute monarchy similar to that of Louis XIV's France.

James' daughters from his first wife, Mary and Anne, were raised as Protestants. Mary married the Protestant Prince of the Dutch Republic, William of Orange, who was James' nephew. On 30 June 1688, a group of Protestant nobles invited Orange to come to England, depose James, and claim the crown of England in the name of his Protestant Stuart wife. William accepted & invaded. This event is known as the 'Glorious Revolution'.

Having no desire to make James a martyr, the Prince of Orange let James escape to Catholic France, and declared that James had abandoned the throne. In France James was received by his cousin and ally, Louis XIV, the most powerful monarch in Europe. Louis established James at his old palace at St Germains.
'The Sun King' planned to use James for his own ends. France was at war with the League of Augsburg, which was established in order to check French power and expansion in Europe. The League mostly comprised Protestant nations, and became known as 'The Grand Alliance' after the inclusion of England under William of Orange.

Louis encouraged James to go to Ireland in order to reclaim his crown. His intention was for James to keep William tied down in Ireland, and English troops and resources out of the war in Europe, for as long as possible.

During his reign James had sent Richard Talbot, Earl of Tyrconnell, to Ireland as Lord Deputy. Tyrconnell placed Catholics in positions of control, purged the army of Protestants, and raised an Irish Catholic army for James. When news of James' expected arrival reached Ireland the Catholics of the country began to raise their heads as the promise of liberty, and prosperity appeared to lie once again under the banner of a Stuart.

12 March 1689, James II lands at Kinsale.

With him arrive French officers, & Irish exiles.

Among the French is Louis XIV's ambassador, Count d'Avaux.

I'll guide James in the interests of France.

Now is the time to strike for Ireland, and the old religion

Patrick Sarsfield returns from France with Irish refugees.

Merci mes amis!

MOOO MOOO

BAAAAAA

BAAAAAA

MOOO

The people give gifts to the departing French sailors.

WELCOME TO IRELAND MAJESTY.

WHAT'S THE PRESENT SITUATION?

JUSTIN MCCARTHY HAS SUBDUED BANDON, WHILE PATRICK SARSFIELD MOVES TO SECURE CONNACHT. RICHARD HAMILTON HAS BEEN SENT TO PACIFY ULSTER.

RESISTANCE IN ULSTER IS WIDESPREAD, BUT CENTRED AROUND DERRY, ENNISKILLEN, & SLIGO.

A CATHOLIC ARMY OF ALMOST 50,000 HAS BEEN RAISED FOR HIS MAJESTY'S SERVICE.

20,000 MUSKETS HAVE BEEN DISTRIBUTED AMONGST THEM, MOST OF WHICH ARE OLD & USELESS.

THE PROTESTANT FORCES ARE WELL ARMED, WHEREAS WE LACK SUPPLIES, & MONEY TO PAY THE ARMY.

YOUR SERVICES ARE ACKNOWLEDGED. I HEREBY ELEVATE YOU TO DUKE OF TYRCONNELL.

IT APPEARS THERE'S A GREAT DEAL OF GOODWILL IN IRELAND FOR ME, BUT LITTLE MEANS TO EXECUTE IT.

FORWARD MARCH!

JUSTIN McCARTHY
I PRESUME?

CORRECT
AMBASSADOR
D'AVAUX

I MERELY
FOLLOW ORDERS.

I'M TOLD YOU'RE
A CAPABLE OFFICER.

YOUR MEN ARE
MOST IMPRESSIVE.

NONE ARE
BELOW 5FT 10.

KING LOUIS, HAS AGREED
TO PROVIDE JAMES WITH
SEASONED FRENCH TROOPS
IN RETURN FOR AN EQUAL
AMOUNT OF IRISH.

IF KING JAMES
APPROVES I'D BE HONOURED.

I WANT YOU TO COMMAND
THIS IRISH BRIGADE
IN FRANCE'S SERVICE.

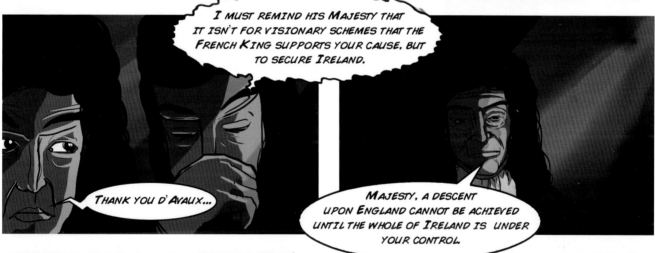

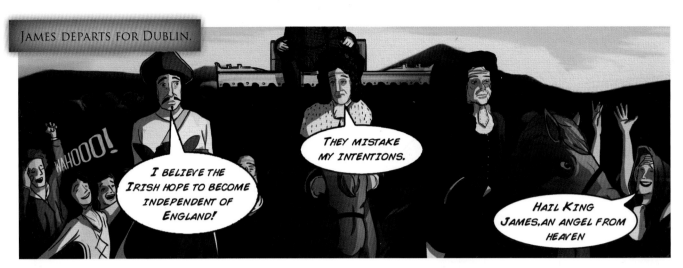

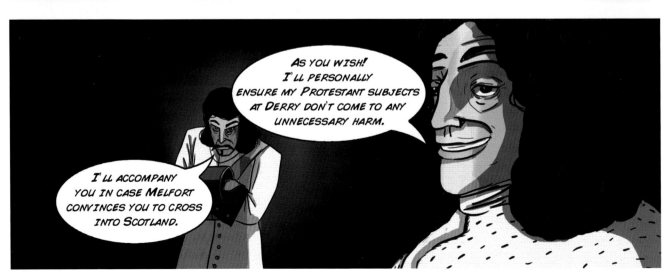

8

WE PRESENT TO HIS MAJESTY THIS ACT OF REPEAL, WHICH ABOLISHES THE CROMWELLIAN ACT OF SETTLEMENT, & RESTORES THE LAND TO ITS RIGHTFUL OWNERS.

IF I SIGN THIS MY PROTESTANT SUBJECTS WILL NEVER FORGIVE ME.

KING LOUIS ASKS YOU TO RESTORE YOUR LOYAL SUBJECTS LANDS!

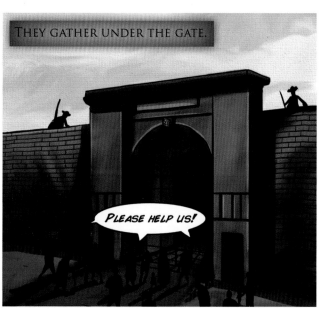

13

Soon Derry starves.

A fleet arrives from England with supplies.

They attempt to relieve the city.

BOOM
BOOM
BOOM

But are badly damaged, & retreat.

JUSTIN MCCARTHY, NOW LORD MOUNTCASHEL, IS ORDERED TO ATTACK ENNISKILLEN.

WE MUST CONTROL CRUM CASTLE BEFORE ATTACKING ENNISKILLEN.

MOUNTCASHEL SENDS THE CAVALRY AHEAD OF HIS MAIN INFANTRY FORCE TO SCOUT.

AT ENNISKILLEN.

SIR, JACOBITE FORCES ATTACKED CRUM CASTLE, & ARE ADVANCING!

TO ARMS! WE'LL MEET THEM ON THE FIELD, & AVOID A SIEGE.

MOUNTCASHEL'S CAVALRY ARE TAKEN BY SURPRISE.

CRACK

CRACK

15

WHEEL RIGHT! REJOIN THE MAIN ARMY!

WHIIZZZZ

THE JACOBITE CAVALRY SHAMEFULLY RUN FOR THEIR LIVES.

NEAR NEWTOWNBUTLER.

FORM UP! PREPARE TO FIGHT!

WE ENCOUNTERED THE ENEMY, BUT THE ENTIRE CAVALRY GALLOPED OFF THE FIELD!

THE ENNISKILLENERS TAKE CASUALTIES.

BOOM! BOOM! BOOM!

BUT OUTMANOEUVRE MOUNTCASHEL'S INFANTRY.

STAND FIRM MEN, HOLD YOUR GROUND!

NO POPERY!

WE'RE TAKING YOU PRISONER TO ENNISKILLEN.

WE MUST RELIEVE THE CITY AT ALL COSTS.

At Derry the Dartmouth frigate braves the pass.

HIT THEM YOU FOOLS!

SPLASH

THEY PASS CULMORE FORT UNDAMAGED.

THEIR GUNNERS MUST BE DRUNK WITH BRANDY!

THE CREW DISMANTLE THE BARRIER.

HORAAAAAH!

AFTER NEARLY FOUR MONTHS DERRY IS RELIEVED.

THE DEMORALISED JACOBITES RETURN TO LEINSTER.

THESE TROOPS ARE UTTERLY RUINED. IT'S USELESS TO EXPECT ANYTHING MORE FROM THEM.

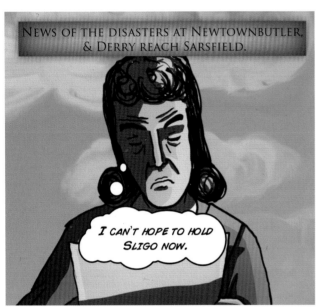

18

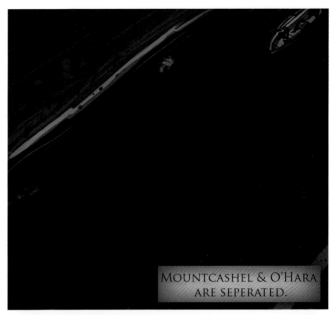

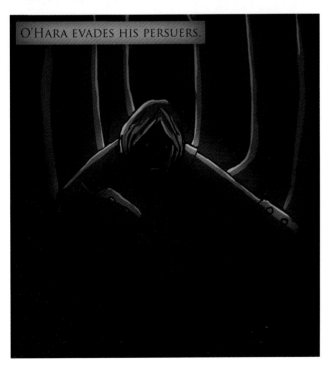

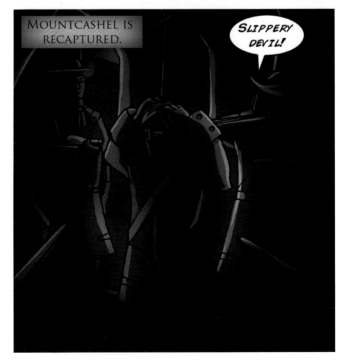

At Dublin Castle.

MELFORT HAS RECEIVED 250,000 FRANCS FOR THAT PURPOSE.

TYRCONNELL, YOU MUST FORMALLY DEMAND MELFORT'S DISMISSAL.

COUNT D'AVAUX, WHAT OF THE MONEY KING LOUIS SENT? MY COMMANDERS HAVEN'T RECEIVED A PENNY OF IT!

MELFORT FAILS TO SEND SUPPLIES, CAUSING TERRIBLE MISHAPS.

D'Avaux confronts James.

MAJESTY, I CAN GET NO ACCOUNT FROM YOUR RECEIVER AS TO WHAT HE'S DONE WITH THE MONEY SUPPLIED BY FRANCE.

MELFORT IS USELESS. HE TURNS A DEAF EAR TO THE REQUESTS OF THE IRISH OFFICERS.

I'M AWARE OF HIS SHORTCOMINGS, & WOULD REMOVE HIM IF THERE WAS ANY ONE ELSE TO PUT IN HIS PLACE.

SURELY IT'S BETTER TO HAVE NO MINISTER THAN TO RETAIN ONE WHO'S CLEARLY INJURING THE KING'S CAUSE.

I URGE YOU TO DO WHAT BENEFITS IRELAND, & FRANCE.

TYRCONNELL HAS ALSO ASKED FOR HIS REMOVAL. MELFORT WILL BE DISMISSED BEFORE THE IRISH OFFICERS ASSASSINATE HIM.

13 AUGUST 1689, WILLIAM SENDS THE DUKE OF SCHOMBERG TO IRELAND.

HIS ARMY IS SWELLED BY THE MILITIAS OF DERRY & ENNISKILLEN.

KING WILLIAM WANTS US TO DEFEAT THE JACOBITES IN A SINGLE PITCHED BATTLE.

SCHOMBERG MARCHES ON DUBLIN.

I WON'T BE WALKED OUT OF IRELAND WITHOUT A FIGHT!

JAMES SETS OUT TO STOP HIM.

BOTH FORCES MEET AT DUNDALK.

24

YOU SQUANDER EVERY CHANCE OF KEEPING THE WILLIAMITES OUT OF IRELAND!

IF I ONLY HAD 6 FRENCH BATTALIONS I'D HAVE DESTROYED SCHOMBERG.

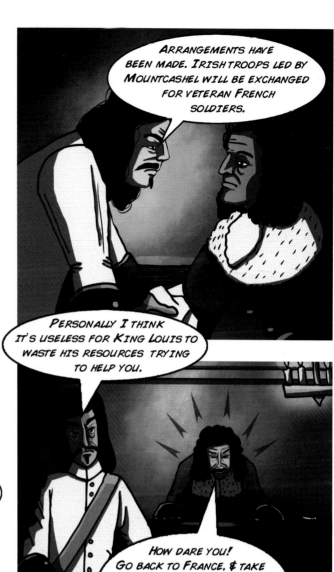

ARRANGEMENTS HAVE BEEN MADE. IRISH TROOPS LED BY MOUNTCASHEL WILL BE EXCHANGED FOR VETERAN FRENCH SOLDIERS.

PERSONALLY I THINK IT'S USELESS FOR KING LOUIS TO WASTE HIS RESOURCES TRYING TO HELP YOU.

HOW DARE YOU! GO BACK TO FRANCE, & TAKE DE ROSEN WITH YOU. IF HE WAS MY SUBJECT I'D HANG HIM FOR HIS CONDUCT AT DERRY!

COUNT DE LAUZUN WILL ARRIVE WITH THE FRENCH TROOPS TO ASSUME SUPREME COMMAND.

JAMES DESCENDS INTO MOODY INACTIVITY.

SCHOMBERG'S REFUSAL TO FIGHT IS A MORAL VICTORY. NOTHING LEFT TO DO NOW, BUT WAIT FOR LAUZUN.

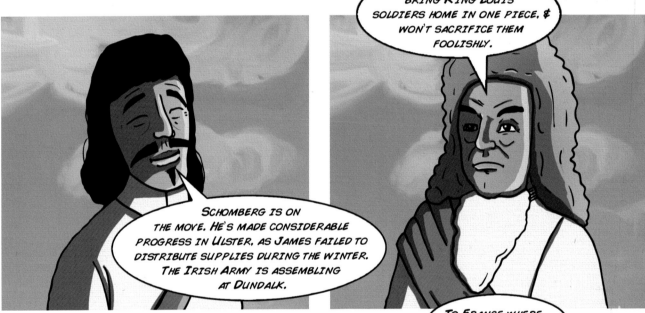

After settling his affairs in England, William of Orange arrives at Carrickfergus on June 14, 1690.

His army consists of Protestant forces from all over Europe.

Joined by Schomberg, William marches his combined force south.

IRELAND IS A PLENTIFUL COUNTRY WORTH FIGHTING FOR.

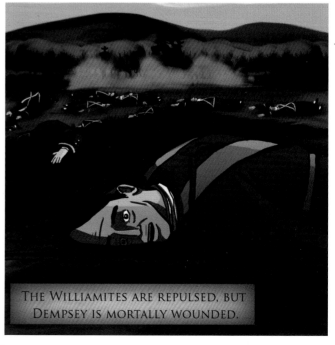

28

30

JAMES PLACES THE CENTRE OF HIS ARMY BY THE CROSSINGS AT OLDBRIDGE.

SIR NIALL O'NEILL IS SENT TO GUARD ROSSNAREE ON THE ARMY'S LEFT.

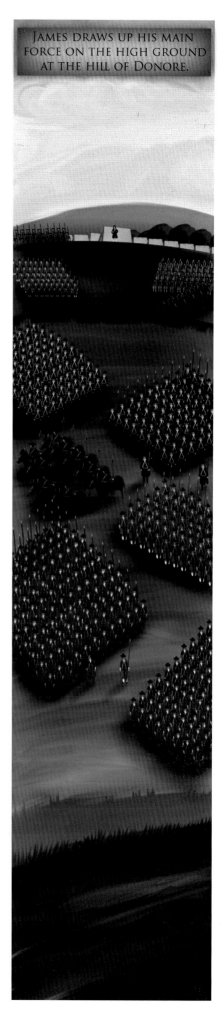

JAMES DRAWS UP HIS MAIN FORCE ON THE HIGH GROUND AT THE HILL OF DONORE.

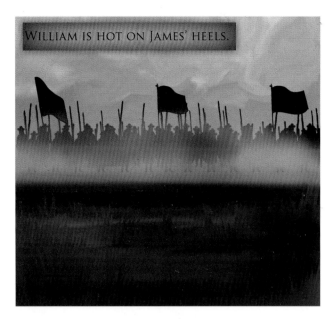

William is hot on James' heels.

He rides down to the riverside.

I need to get a better look at James' camp.

Sarsfield spots him from the other side.

That's Orange! Bring some artillery, now!

BOOM BOOM

KA-BOOM

WHIZ

It could've come closer.

WILLIAM SENDS 10,000 HORSE & FOOT
TO CROSS AT ROSSNAREE.

SCHOMBERG IS TO LEAD THE MAIN
ATTACK AT OLDBRIDGE.

ORANGE MOVES EAST TOWARDS
DROGHEDA TO FIND ANOTHER CROSSING.

AT ROSSNAREE.

BRACE YOURSELVES.

SIR, THE WILLIAMITES APPROACH IN FORCE!

O'NEILL'S MEN BRAVELY HOLD OUT FOR AN HOUR.

KING JAMES, THE WILLIAMITES HAVE FORCED THE CROSSING AT ROSSNAREE! THEY MUST BE STOPPED!

THERE'S TOO MANY, RETREAT!

WE'LL BE FLANKED!

JAMES LEADS THE MAJORITY OF HIS ARMY AWAY FROM OLDBRIDGE TO CHECK THE ADVANCE.

HE ENCOUNTERS THEM AT AN IMPASSABLE RAVINE.

THE DEVIL HIMSELF COULDN'T GET THROUGH!

TYRCONNELL ORDERS THE CAVALRY TO ATTACK.

THEY SMASH THE WILLIAMITE LINES.

COME ON, THERE ARE YOUR PERSECUTORS!

SCHOMBERG RALLIES HIS MEN.

TARGET THEIR GENERAL!

SCHOMBERG IS KILLED.

37

WILLIAM CROSSES THE BOYNE
WITH HIS CAVALRY.

THE REMAINING JACOBITES
AT OLDBRIDGE ARE
OVERWHELMED.

JAMES TAKES FLIGHT.

I'M NOT
STAYING IN IRELAND
FOREVER!

THE FRENCH INFANTRY, & IRISH DRAGOONS
COVER THE JACOBITE RETREAT.

BACK AT DUBLIN.

I ADVISED HIM TO LEAVE FOR FRANCE TO PREVENT HIS FALLING INTO THE ENEMY'S HANDS.

WHERE'S KING JAMES?

JAMES HAS LEFT US TO DECIDE WHETHER TO MAKE PEACE WITH ORANGE, OR CONTINUE THE WAR.

THE IRISH REGROUP AT LIMERICK.

I SHOULD MAKE PEACE WHILE GOOD CONDITIONS CAN BE OBTAINED.

THIS CITY CAN BE TAKEN BY A BOMBARDMENT OF ROASTED APPLES!

I'M LEAVING WITH MY REGIMENTS FOR GALWAY. FROM THERE WE'LL RETURN TO FRANCE.

JAMES IS GONE, & THERE'S NO GLORY TO BE HAD FOR THEM IN IRELAND NOW. I'LL ESCORT YOU WITH MY TROOPS.

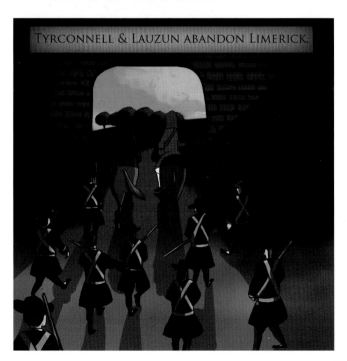

TYRCONNELL & LAUZUN ABANDON LIMERICK.

SARSFIELD & GOVERNOR BOISSELEAU REMAIN TO DEFEND THE CITY.

SURRENDER TO ORANGE ISN'T AN OPTION. WE'LL PUT OUR BACKS TO THESE WALLS, & FIGHT FOR THE ENTIRE KINGDOM.

39

9 AUGUST 1690, ORANGE COMES BEFORE LIMERICK.

DIG THE TRENCHES, ERECT THE BATTERIES...

ORANGE HAS CALLED FOR OUR SURRENDER.

LETS EARN HIS RESPECT BY A VIGOROUS DEFENCE.

A WILLIAMITE DESERTER CLAIMS THAT ORANGE HAS SENT FOR HIS SIEGE ARTILLERY.

THE CITY'S FATE IS SEALED WITH ITS ARRIVAL.

THEN IT MUST BE INTERCEPTED.

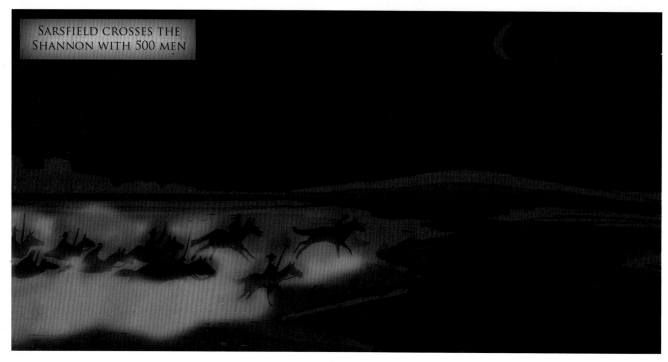

SARSFIELD CROSSES THE SHANNON WITH 500 MEN

40

42

43

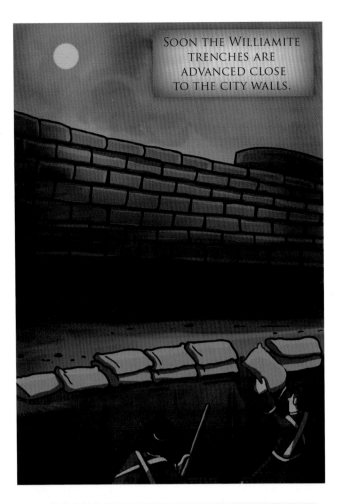

SOON THE WILLIAMITE TRENCHES ARE ADVANCED CLOSE TO THE CITY WALLS.

THE ARTILLERY FROM WATERFORD HAS MADE A BREACH.

THE DEFENDERS ARE PREPARED FOR THE ASSAULT.

THEY WAIT ANXIOUSLY FOR THE CARNAGE TO COMMENCE.

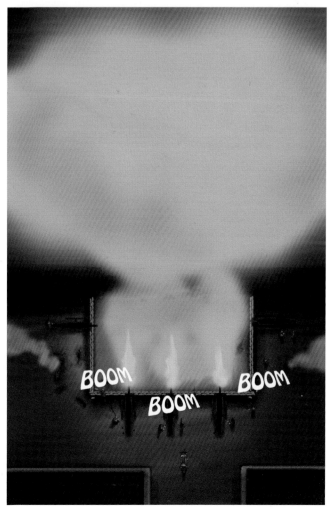

46

War of the Two Kings

Orange departs Ireland leaving General de Ginkel in charge of his army in Ireland. William's army was badly bloodied at Limerick having lost close to 3,000 men throughout the siege. Both sides go into winter quarters, & William's army loses another 2,000 men to disease.

The French fleet arrive in Galway to convey the French regiments and officers back to France. The success at Limerick gives Tyrconnell new hope, and he decides to go to France with the fleet in order to personally appeal to Louis and James for further aid to continue the war in Ireland.

In September 1690 Cork and Kinsale are captured in a daring series of attacks by the combined Williamite navy and land forces. Over 5,000 troops and ample supplies are lost. The landing of future French aid is seriously impeded, as Limerick and Galway are the only ports left in Irish hands. These events ended the campaigns of 1689-1690. William of Orange and James Stuart never set foot in Ireland again.

moccupress

www.moccupress.com